RESISTANCE RISING

America's Hope in 2026 and 2028

JOE GALLINA
SANFORD HOLST

RESISTANCE
PRESS LLC

Resistance Press LLC
1141 E. Glendale Avenue #1158
Phoenix, AZ 85020

Liberty Bell attribution Captain Theberge, NOAA, cc-by-2.0. Soldier Silhouette Free Vector Download.

Publisher's Cataloging-In-Publication Data

Gallina, Joe and Sanford Holst
Resistance rising : America's hope in 2026 and 2028 / Joe Gallina and Sanford Holst.

pages : cm
Includes bibliographical references and index.
ISBN: 979-8-9953921-0-1 (paperback)
ISBN: 979-8-9953921-1-8 (eBook)

Library of Congress Control Number 2026940203

Liberty Bell

Preface

Most special elections in 2026 have been won by Democrats and Independents.

See how it has been done, and try this in your own neighborhood to make a real difference.

The first essential ingredient has been to keep the focus on Donald Trump's mountain of disasters for the American people.

Then it has been necessary to shift the emphasis from stacks of money to personal contacts. The main part of this has been to reawaken concern in voters for the things most important to *them*.

Attention has had to be given to the many people who sat out past elections thinking it would not affect their life. Getting them involved right away has made a huge difference.

And of course, the Democratic influencers and commentators have had to keep the Resistance energy flowing into people every day, swelling the ranks of these campaigns nationwide.

Other people are using these things to make miracles happen around you. Now you can be part of the miracle.

Contents

Chapter

One

Enough Is Enough

Rain poured down outside Marisa's home in Oklahoma City on a Thursday morning in April of 2025. She was taking care of her three children and had no way of knowing all of hell's fury was about to come crashing through her front door.

Marisa was just a mom in an average American family getting her kids settled in this rented home in the heartland of America. They had just moved from Maryland, and her husband was still back there, finishing up some things. He would join her in a few days.

The explosion of noise as her front door was shattered threw Marisa into panic. She immediately tried to protect her children from the roughly twenty men armed with guns who forced their way in and occupied every room of the house. They identified themselves as federal agents with the U.S. Marshals, ICE and the FBI. They began tearing the place apart and they started taking her family's personal belongings.

She pleaded with them, asking, "What are you doing here? What's happening?"

One of the armed men curtly replied, "We have a warrant for the house, a search warrant."

She told them she and her children were citizens. She kept repeating, "We're citizens!" They didn't care.

The men ordered Marisa and her daughters outside into the rain before they could even put on clothes.

"They wanted me to change in front of all of them, in between all of them," she said. "My husband has not even seen my daughter in her undergarments—her own dad, because it's respectful. You have her out there, a minor, in her underwear."

The names on the warrant were not those of anyone in her family. She recognized the names as being on mail that still arrived at the house. Again, the men didn't care.

Even knowing this was the wrong family, the men took all their phones, laptops and their life savings in cash as "evidence."

"I told them before they left, I said you took my phone. We have no money. I just moved here," she said. "I have to feed my children. I'm going to need gas money. I need to be able to get around. Like, how do you just leave me like this? Like an abandoned dog."[1]

That actually happened in America. It started after Donald Trump began issuing his waves of executive orders. And with different variations it has happened again and again across the country. Life in the United States has been changing at an incredibly rapid pace.

The same month Marisa's door was broken down in Oklahoma, ICE in New York swooped in to capture a teenager, but picked up the wrong one. They decided to take him anyway. He was deported to El Salvador's notorious super prison.[2]

Again, *in the same month* but this time out West in Arizona, a U.S. citizen was wrongfully arrested by border patrol south of Tucson. He was held for almost ten days until his family showed up with proof of citizenship.[3] The man was treated as guilty until proven innocent. In America.

As a journalist and commentator in Washington, DC, I have seen many things over the years. But what happened to these people seems almost impossible in this land where we grew up believing in "liberty and justice for all."

The stories that pass through my hands every day bear an ever-increasing amount of pain from Trump's executive orders. They are hitting Americans in all walks of life. The stories are told by veterans, senior citizens, women, LGBTQ+, judges, university students, people with health problems and many others. It's true that all of these people and their situations are different. But they do seem to share one thing in common: a desire to make the pain stop.

I remember when the resistance to Trump's actions began in 2016 on the day he was elected to his first term of office. Leah Greenberg and Ezra Levin, who were two young people working at political staff positions in Washington, DC, were among the first to respond. They began assembling a pamphlet for people inclined to resist and called it "Indivisible Guide."

They distributed their guide online as a Google Doc to make it as widely accessible as possible. It simply urged people to organize locally and pressure elected officials to oppose Trump's agenda. From this small beginning the major "Indivisible" organization has been quickly growing. This added backbone to the long-standing Democratic Club framework but with a new and energetic purpose.

In January of 2017 we all remember Trump's inauguration and his fake news claims of having more people show up than came to Obama's inauguration, despite many pictures to the contrary. I was busy that same day getting my Facebook page up for *Call to Activism*. It was just a place for people to blow off steam about Trump, and find encouragement to become more active resisting his actions.

But as Trump caused ever more pain for people, I began to pour more and more hours into *Call to Activism*. Even so I never imagined it would one day be carried on nine social media platforms and involve six million people. It even added the "Take a Friend to Vote" idea which has been adding a new dimension to this campaign season.

In those early days Alexandria Ocasio-Cortez, now popularly known as AOC, was still a waitress at a bar in New York City. But the next year she ran for Congress and shocked everyone by winning. Ever since then she has been one of the most active resisters possible. Her reliance on small contributions to fund her own campaign helped to popularize the "Time or the Dime" approach to balanced funding. Then her wildly successful Fight Oligarchy Tour in 2025 expanded the subject of how the rich should be helping the poor, not themselves.

Many other activists have also gotten caught up in the new things going on, including Rachel

Maddow, Mark Cuban, the Meiselas Brothers and many others.

To be honest, back in those early days the loose Resistance consisted of whoever wanted to join, and they did whatever they wanted to do. But we learned. By 2020 some of our efforts were paying off. Joe Biden won the presidency, and life was good. But the far right regrouped. Their networks exploded, and after Elon Musk bought Twitter the playing field tilted hard against us.

The re-election of Trump in 2024—and his horrible presidential orders on inauguration day—were a real slap upside the head. It became clear we all had to do better. What arose from that setback was not the old Resistance. It was a leaner, louder, smarter force, one ready to face the next fight and the one after that. The resilient network we call Resistance 2.0 was well and truly born.

When Americans suffer at the hands of the government, our usual source of protection has always been the elected officials representing us in the U.S. Senate and House of Representatives. But where has that help gone?

Republicans in Congress have rushed to do Trump's bidding, and Democrats have struggled. The president's Cabinet members are a prime example. They are supposed to be held to a high standard by having them confirmed in the U.S. Senate. But when Trump appointed some grossly unqualified Cabinet members, several of them received Democratic votes. That was unconscionable. Kristi Noem was nominated to be Secretary of Homeland Security. Seven Democrats voted for her.[4] She became leader of the ICE—the same ICE which then set about detaining and deporting U.S. citizens. Where was the opposition and resistance which was supposed to hold Trump to account and limit his excesses? It has been nowhere to be seen.

Actions like those have forced individual people and members of the Resistance to step up and fill the void.

In late January of 2025 a random Reddit post started a unique chain of events. It proposed having 50 demonstrations against Trump in 50 states on 1 day. The idea caught on. So people started organizing themselves into a group called 50501. Resistance leaders all across the board began supporting these proposed demonstrations. The result was magical.

I was part of a "Hands Off" rally held on April 5 of 2025. Almost four million people showed up from coast to coast. Then we all got together to promote an even bigger "No Kings Day" rally on June 14. About five million people took to the streets to oppose Trump and his authoritarian-style military parade. People were upset and ready to show it.

Even so, the Resistance was more than a few highly visible rallies.

Our work has impacted voting in special elections across the country. These happen whenever someone in federal or state elected office dies or retires. Remarkably enough, Democrats have been polling 10% higher than usual in these special elections. That is an incredible change, even in an "up" year for one party or the other.

One of these special elections became front-page news. Elon Musk made personal appearances and spent $21 million to push an open Wisconsin supreme court seat into the MAGA column and create a conservative majority. He failed miserably. The Resistance turned out in full force and the liberal candidate, Susan Crawford, won walking away, with a 10% victory margin.

The much-welcomed message from this experience was that money is important in political races, but people-power is much more effective. We'll see more on this later.

Among Trump's many disasters in the White House, starting the Iran War has to be one for the ages. Iran is a long-time enemy of ours, just like Russia or China. But the President is not allowed to start a war with Russia, China or anyone else without approval from Congress. The same is true with Iran.

But in 2026 Trump did it anyway. And without any Democratic or Republican guidance beforehand. So he kept blundering into unseen situations. That created maddeningly higher prices—especially at gas pumps—and cost American lives. This will get a deeper look since it affects so many other things.

Millions of irate individuals of all political stripes have joined and quickly influenced the actions of the Resistance. I've had the pleasure of working with many leaders among them, and now pass along the stories of twenty of those remarkable individuals here.

See how the growing strength of the Resistance gives Democrats a chance, and maybe even an edge, going into the trial by fire expected in the 2026 and 2028 elections.

Chapter

Two

Take a Friend to Vote

Even I was surprised by the possibility of Democrats having some kind of advantage going into the elections in 2026 and 2028.

This was closely related to one of the strangest facts from the 2024 presidential election: that Kamala Harris pulled in 75 million votes, Donald Trump won slightly more than that, and *82 million eligible Americans did not vote!*[5,6]

Since MAGA voters are very good about getting to the polls, most of those lazy voters were anti-Trump ballots. That is where Trump won the election. The Resistance is not making that same mistake in 2026 and 2028.

In special elections a strong appeal is being made to disaffected voters who thought voting did not affect their lives. Trump's many disasters have shown how important each vote is.

And nationwide we are bringing in more voters because we have a special advantage. Resistance leaders such as the ones in these pages have between 1 and 31 million followers EACH. We communicate directly with these interested voters. Even if these rousing voices only draw tens of millions of good people to action, that is enough to turn the tide in the current elections.

Take a Friend

Cosima and I were there when the whole idea of Take a Friend to Vote began during the Biden years. Times were so good in those days, it didn't really seem necessary to pursue it. But then came the Trump circus of disasters in 2025 and the influence of these missing people in our elections became too obvious.

Even the extreme partisanship which has taken root in recent years has not been an obstacle. We have so many "sometime" voters wating in the wings that to win all we need do is get them to the polls.

Take a Friend to Vote has shown us how to do this the right way. And it's so easy!

1. Keep an eye open for someone who did not vote in the past 1 or 2 elections.
2. Ask how they feel about Trump.
3. If this person missed an election and does''t like Trump, you've found a new "friend".
4. If they're not registered to vote, help them notify the right office.
5. If absentee ballots are allowed in your area, help them sign up for it.
6. Keep in touch with them socially until election time, then offer them a voting party: both of you vote at the same time, and you treat them to a nice dessert or other fun thing afterward.
   - By mailing your absentee ballots at the same time, or
   - By going to an "early voting" polling place in your area and voting, or
   - By going on election day to their polling place with them, it's all done!

Compare this to the usual voter registration drives (which I've done many times). These ask you to spend many weekends on a sidewalk interrupting strangers and asking if they want to register. And if they do register, you don't know if you just added another MAGA vote. If you're lucky enough to register an anti-Trump voter, there is no way to know if they will ever vote. People who have to be talked into registering don't always vote.

The other alternative is to contribute many hundreds of dollars to candidates who will usually spend it on advertising, which rarely changes anyone's vote, nor gets them to their polling place.

Take a Friend to Vote simply involves you and one other person of your choosing. It's done at any time convenient to you. It's a guaranteed vote for the good guys. And you get to enjoy half the treat of chocolate, pastry, frozen yogurt or whatever else that may be.

The best part is you're doing it alongside thousands or of millions of other Resisters in local or national elections. And on election night you can be all smiles watching everything on your TV.

I am *so* looking forward to that. And have already picked out my did-not-vote friend.

Let's do this thing!

Chapter

Three

The Time or the Dime

For many people there really is a question of "who the hell has enough time to spend on all these political issues?"

It's true that the fate of our family and our country hang in the balance. And that's heavy stuff. We really want to help. But what can we do?

Actually, if that's the case, there are a couple of things you could do. Traditionally, we've been expected to just send large amounts of cash and hope for the best. But as Trump has shown, we sometimes get the worst.

On the other hand, Susan Crawford, the Wisconsin supreme court judge, showed a different way to do it. When Elon Musk donated millions of dollars trying to shut her down, she asked people to give their time and won spectacularly.

Maybe it's time to consider the personal approach of interacting with voters. In special elections held all across the country this past year, personal contact seems to have been one of the major factors affecting people's votes.

Seeing someone at your front door who is upset enough about rising costs, presidential transgressions, legislative inactivity, and judicial complicity seems to have gotten a strong reaction. People decide to get upset too—at least upset enough to get out and vote.

You have to see it actually happening to fully appreciate it. And hopefully you will experience this yourself by seeing it take place in real life. It may even be happening right in your own state, because all Congressional Representatives and 35 of all Senators are up for grabs in each two-year balloting cycle.

When these elections are held in nearby congressional offices you could make your presence felt this year. Even if you are satisfied with your own person in Congress, you can still be active and affect the vote nearby.

A neighboring Red senator could feel severe heat this way. If you're looking for something interesting to do on your next vacation, find a Red senator and ask their Blue competitor where they could use some help. Then go spend some time there with voters and make a real difference. Accomplish something that you can see reflected on the evening news for years to come.

If you haven't got the time to go there yourself, maybe just give the dime.

In other words, consider buying your way out of all those hours of work by donating money to the right places so other people put in the long hours of work to keep the heavy wheels of liberty rolling forward.

How much would all those hours of manual labor be worth, really? It's probably much more than the few hundred dollars that goes into election donation plates.

In that case, instead of doing that work in person, maybe send a few thousand in proper investments. And place it with a congressional or senatorial office where it will be felt the most. Have a real impact this year.

And one way you can definitely have an effect this time is by taking a friend to vote. This is especially true if your "friend" lives in a Red district.

If you know someone who did not vote last time because of school, work, personal commitments or other reasons, make a date with them to vote. You can both walk together to the polls by cell phone, even if you are in different districts.

Remember, if you can't give the time, give the dime.

Democratic
Influencers
1 thru 4

Alexandria Ocasio-Cortez, Leah Greenberg, Ezra Levin, Mark Cuban & Joe Gallina

For the 20 influential people in the Resistance we visit here, you may already know their name. But do you know their game?

Their millions of followers on social media are shown at the time of this writing. Their handle (@name) is usually the same on all media, but if it varies, this is their Bluesky handle.

Alexandria Ocasio-Cortez

31.0 million

@aoc

Popularly known as AOC, she is a NY congresswoman and prominent progressive Democrat.

AOC never tires of mentioning her working roots in the gritty Bronx neighborhood of New York City. She makes a point of representing working people rather than corporate fat cats—and can say that more convincingly than most elected people.

It is fair to say her first election victory stunned the entire country. She was running in a solidly Democratic Congressional district against a ten-term incumbent who was chair of the Democratic Caucus, a very powerful position in Washington, DC. He also had $1.5 million to spend, compared to the $83,000 AOC could muster. She not only was still waiting tables and tending bar during the campaign, she proudly declared, "For 80 percent of this campaign, I operated out of a paper grocery bag hidden behind that bar."[7] She won that election anyway. And the ones that came after it.

To make a long story short, AOC is a *very* persuasive person.

She is also unwaveringly proud of her Puerto Rican roots. Her father had Puerto Rican ancestry, though he was born in the Bronx. Her mother was born in Puerto Rico and, yes, people there are U.S.

citizens at birth. If AOC eventually moves to higher office there will likely be no end of "birther" conspiracy theories around her.

I doubt she will care. AOC revels in her heritage and enjoys throwing Hispanic phrases into her comments. ¡Tú puedes, chica!

It didn't seem possible that her public attention could rise any higher, but then she went on the Fight Oligarchy Tours of the United States with Senator Bernie Sanders in 2025. He did the first few appearances by himself, but when she joined him things really took off. There was publicity galore because they were taking the fight to Red strongholds as well as some safely Blue states.

The turnouts were fantastic! Records were set in many cities for political crowd size. Venues overflowed so much that in most cases AOC and Sanders had to go out afterwards and give unscheduled talks to the thousands waiting outside in the open air to hear them.

When you got it, you got it.

Leah Greenberg/Ezra Levin

2.3 million

@indivisible.org

The Indivisible political organization was their brainchild in 2016 and it has spread across America.

Every Thursday, Indivisible co-founders Leah Greenberg and Ezra Levin meet on-line with their members to wade through the week's news, answer questions, and provide timely calls to action.

Then members divide up nationwide to pursue issues of local interest. They also come together on issues of national interest. This caused a natural merging of interests with 50501 on more massive, national campaigns in protest of Trump's bizarre actions.

Leah and Ezra met at Carleton College when he was a senior and she was a junior, but their promising futures were quickly tested. He was called away to AmeriCorps VISTA in San Jose, California, but left a year later to come to Washington, DC, and work for Congressman Lloyd Doggett.

Also in 2008, Leah graduated and headed for Washington, DC, becoming a lobbyist for Humanity United. They both pursued many left-of-center interests, but finally decided they could not put off the inevitable any longer. Leah and Ezra were married in 2015.

She burnished her credentials by earning a Masters in Law and Diplomacy from the Fletcher School at Tufts University. Ezra added a Masters in Public Affairs from Princeton School of Public and International Affairs.

In response to Trump's election and disastrous deeds, they founded Indivisible in 2016.

Mark Cuban

14.9 million
@mcuban
Left-leaning businessman worth $6 billion and a long-time host on the TV program Shark Tank.

Mark may be one of the most "centrist" people in the political world. With all his business skills and the billions of dollars he has amassed, one would expect him to be a devoted Republican clamoring to get more wealth for himself. But he also cares about people, and believes people as rich as himself should pay their fair share.

What kind of man is he? As an owner of the Dallas Mavericks basketball team, he was concerned when a former player of his became homeless. He eventually convinced the player, Delonte West, to meet him at a gas station. They talked, and the man agreed to accept a hotel room and let Mark pay for treatment at a drug rehabilitation center.[8] If a few stray people had not caught video clips of this, no one would have known it happened. Some people talk the talk, Mark walks the walk.

He has sometimes considered running for public office, but so far has never taken that step. He made his political feelings abundantly clear in 2016, though.

> Billionaire sports and TV mogul Mark Cuban formally endorsed Hillary Clinton on Saturday at a campaign stop in Pittsburgh.
>
> Introducing Clinton and running mate Tim Kaine in his hometown, Cuban called out Donald Trump, saying, "Leadership is not yelling and screaming and intimidating.
>
> "You know what we call a person like that in Pittsburgh? A jagoff," Cuban continued. "Is there any bigger jagoff in the world than Donald Trump?"[9]
>
> *Politico*
> *July 30, 2016*

Oh, and it's probably worth noting that he tends to speak his mind.

Joe Gallina

6.0 million
@joegallina
@calltoactivism
His "Call to Activism" is now popular on virtually all social media platforms.

Joe was an attorney practicing in Maryland when Trump took office in January of 2017. The explosion of fake news from the White House seemed to be getting little pushback from traditional media, so he decided to jump into the fray with an activist page on Facebook, *Call to Activism.*

What began as a simple outlet quickly grew into a national platform, with people piling on from all over the country trying to make sense of what was happening. Today his wife Cosima runs Facebook operations for the network and frequently joins Joe in interviews, making *Call to Activism* a true partnership both on and off camera.

This was a natural fit for Joe, because he had started his legal career with the Department of Justice and knew his way around the halls of power. He had even done volunteer work at the White House Office of Presidential Correspondence. There's an old saying about "it's not what you know, it's who you know." There seems to be something to that.

His ease with the Washington world lets elected officeholders and high-level political officials relax. So they give interviews others would die for. When you go on almost any social media platform you'll see videos of Joe talking with people such as Nancy Pelosi, Hakeem Jeffries, Elizabeth Warren, Governor J.B. Pritzker and many others.

These talks led to the *Daily Mic Drop* series of video clips which excerpt the juiciest parts of those talks for wide dissemination. One choice bit from an interview with House Rep. Jasmine Crockett garnered over five million views.

People seem to enjoy the honesty and immediacy of seeing public officials without teleprompters or speechwriters, just saying what they really believe. Joe and Cosima built a platform where those conversations can reach millions.

Chapter

Four

Economy on Fire

Trump was taking a severe beating on the Epstein sex scandal in July of 2025, with Democrats and MAGA demanding the files be released to the public. So he resorted to his usual tactics: overload and distraction. He had his people roll out demands for an investigation of Barack Obama! As usual, there was no logical reason for this. It was just more furor and headline-grabbing.

Trump is a past-master at keeping a torrent of presidential orders and issues flying around, making it almost impossible to focus on any one critical issue. As a result people opposed to his harmful actions have their attention spread in so many different directions that they can't effectively organize and beat him back on any of them.

After seeing that problem addressed in different parts of the country, the only good answer that presented itself was: don't play the game his way.

We only seem to succeed when focusing on one or two issues at a time. When we win one of those, then we can move on to the next one. And the consensus top issue is the economy.

If you feel another failure on Trump's part should be included, definitely add that to your action list. But certainly this one is huge.

It's the Economy, Stupid!

People across America have been suffering from price increases for many years now, but polls show it is still their #1 concern. If anything, Trump's tariffs and the Iran war have made people's financial problems worse than ever before. And they want an end to it!

This was one of the critical issues that hurt Kamala Harris in 2024. Political polls showed the economy was voters' top concern. Harris and Biden were the incumbents, and people took their anger out on them. Now, after all of Trump's promises to make things better, the economy is even worse.

Do not let him off the hook! He is battering everyone—except the very rich—in so many ways that we need to keep pounding on the following.

The War in Iran

The most flagrant cost in the Iran War was the price at the gas pumps, which shot higher by more than a dollar a gallon. Considering how many gallons go into a gas tank each visit, that can add up quickly. And yes, people noticed every time they drove in.

These costs spread quickly to higher food prices, driven up by higher transportation costs. Government costs shot higher due to a billion dollars a day in highly sophisticated weaponry and bombs dropped on Iran.

And then there was the terrible cost in human lives as bodies draped in American flags came back from the war zone. The prices were high and the pain lasted.

The Tariffs

Virtually everyone seemed to understand tariffs were additional taxes on the people of your own country—except for President Trump. Sure enough, those costs slapped on foreign goods almost immediately reappeared as higher American prices on store shelves.

Many of Trump's own people were seriously hobbled or entirely put out of business by these displacements. But all of us suffered. And the heavy costs of tariffs bobbed up and down continuously as people and nations complained.

Through it all, Trump's search for "free money!" never ended and our pain has continued.

Cutting Public Services

One of Trump's clear targets in cost-cutting has been to reduce or eliminate services to average citizens. In 2026 he cut the Department of Education, the Environmental Protection Agency, various energy and climate projects, the National Institutes of Health and other areas.

These transferred health, education and other burdens directly onto our backs. But they also suddenly put thousands of people out of work with little thought or planning. Unemployment costs were unexpectedly incurred which we had to pay, and some of these people had to take lesser-paying jobs just to keep simple food on their family's table.

Letting economic problems hit working Americans is not new. Bill Clinton famously figured it out in his successful campaign for president, coining the phrase, "It's the economy, stupid!" He and his advisors recognized this was a simple and modest way of reminding themselves that many issues are important, but at that moment in time this was the dominant one with voters.

It was true then, it was true in 2024, and Trump's blundering is still making it true now.

Be relentless. Beat on the painful economy.

Chapter

Five

Facing Money and Power

The bizarre behavior of America's media under Donald Trump is surprisingly similar to the movie *Silence of the Lambs,* where no one would speak up for the innocents being slaughtered. Who is willing to speak up for the millions of people being harmed by Trump's actions? Just look at what is happening with major newspapers today.

Published by
The Guardian
October 23, 2024

> Patrick Soon-Shiong, the billionaire owner of the ***Los Angeles Times***, refused to allow the newspaper's editorial board to endorse Kamala Harris for president, the former editor of the paper's opinion section told a media news outlet on Wednesday.
>
> Mariel Garza, a veteran California journalist who has worked for the *Times'* editorial board for nearly a decade, resigned from the paper in protest of Soon-Shiong's decision….
>
> "In dangerous times, honest people need to stand up. This is how I'm standing up," Garza told CJR.
>
> Soon-Shiong, a biotech billionaire, bought the *Los Angeles Times* in 2018, pledging to make it one of the "bastions of democracy in this country". He said at the time that his $500m purchase of the *Times* and other California papers was an effort to fight fake news….[10]

Sure. He has made it as much of a bastion of democracy as Elon Musk has made X/Twitter.

Could this possibly get any worse?

Yes, it could. The venerable *Washington Post* did virtually the same thing.

Published by CNN

October 25, 2024

For the first time in decades, ***The Washington Post*** will not endorse a candidate in this year's presidential election, the newspaper's publisher announced Friday, a decision that sparked widespread outrage among the paper's staffers.

Robert Kagan, an opinion editor-at-large at the *Post* who resigned Friday in protest after the announcement, said Bezos made the decision to appease Trump.

"This is obviously an effort by Jeff Bezos to curry favor with Donald Trump in the anticipation of his possible victory," Robert Kagan told CNN's *Erin Burnett OutFront*. "Trump has threatened to go after Bezos' business. Bezos runs one of the largest companies in America. They have tremendously intricate relations with the federal government. They depend on the federal government."

The move was also denounced by Marty Baron, the *Post's* former executive editor who led the newspaper through its coverage of the January 6, 2021, attack.

> "This is cowardice, with democracy as its casualty. Donald Trump will see this as an invitation to further intimidate owner Bezos (and others)," Baron wrote in a social media post. "Disturbing spinelessness at an institution famed for courage."[11]

Former editor Marty Baron must be a prophet. Because that is exactly what has happened.

Published by Axios
July 30, 2025

> Paramount, the CBS parent company, paid $16 million this month to settle Trump's lawsuit over the editing of a *60 Minutes* interview with Vice President Kamala Harris during the 2024 campaign. The deal cleared the way for the FCC to approve Paramount's $8 billion merger with Skydance, triggering major backlash from Democrats and press freedom activists. Trump said last week that the settlement is worth more than $36 million, including $20 million in ads, PSAs or "similar" programming from the new owner.[12]

Deference to Trump has caused the established media in the US to essentially give him a free ride ever since election day. All the harsh acts he commits are treated as if they are normal.

Oh, there is an occasional "naughty, naughty" admonition. Then the whole thing is dropped and the media moves on to reporting his next over-the-top executive order.

The impression being given to the public is that Trump will always win, so there is no sense resisting.

I believe otherwise.

Resist like hell!

And if the established media won't do it themselves, we will have to step up in their place. In posts, podcasts, written articles and online videos we have to make sure the word gets out!

Democratic
Influencers
5 thru 8

Rachel Maddow, Stephen King, George Takei & the Meiselas Brothers

Rachel Maddow

15.2 million
@maddow
MS NOW's leading news host, as well as an Emmy and Grammy winner.

Rachel is best known for hosting the *Rachel Maddow Show* on ***MS NOW*** and for being an outspoken liberal. Her posts on social media often reflect her cable TV work, adding nuances to the top stories she is pursuing at that moment.

She also has the distinction of being the first openly lesbian anchor of a major prime-time news program in the US. Even so, LGBTQ+ issues do not dominate her reporting by any means. Yet this is also not avoided when it is legitimately part of the story she is covering. That is a nice mixture which seems to work well with her audiences.

Rachel is undoubtedly smart. Coming out of Stanford she earned a Rhodes scholarship to study at Oxford, graduating five years later with a doctoral degree in politics. So when she covers the news it is from a position of strength, rather than just repeating other people's words.

Farther than just being an outspoken liberal, Rachel has managed to work with deeply-committed conservatives over the years and lived to tell the tale. In 2005 she was a regular panelist on the MSNBC program *Tucker* hosted by Tucker Carlson. She even had a working relationship with Roger

Ailes of *Fox News,* picking up useful bits of tradecraft.

Rachel is undoubtedly one of the leading commentators of the political world.

Stephen King

9.8 million
@stephenking
World-famous author of horror stories, and politically active since Gary Hart's presidential campaign in '84.

Celebrated author of horror novels ever since *Carrie* hit book shelves in 1974, Stephen King also has a strong civic streak that might surprise most people. That might have had to do with his growing up in Maine where his father left the family when Steve was two. He and his brother had to struggle a bit and help their mom, but they got by. He seemed to come through it okay, but somehow struggling and fear seemed to find its way into his writing. And there was something compelling about the way he drew the reader in, among the darkness and the light which he controlled.

Steve has been particularly outspoken about the recent deployment of National Guard troops in Democratic run cities, as well as the gestapo-like tactics employed by ICE to remove undocumented (as well as documented) immigrants. He has warned us that these actions are the hallmark of an authoritarian takeover. Steve is hopeful the silver lining will be that "they could find themselves swamped by a blue wave. America is wising up to the fact that Trump is turning the American dream into a nightmare."

So he seems perfectly comfortable dealing with the horror story that Donald Trump is writing. And give the devil his due, Trump is really convincing at this. It actually feels like we're living through his horror story.

Thank heaven we've got Stephen King on our side, someone who knows his way into and out of terrible circumstances.

George Takei

14.9 million
@georgetakei

Star Trek's Mr. Sulu has been politically active since the 1972 Democratic National Convention.

That young fellow in the science fiction epic series *Star Trek* has made a few laps around the sun since then, but George Takei is still as adventurous and active as ever.

And talk about resilient! George was only five years old when he and his Japanese American parents were imprisoned at an internment camp in

California at the beginning of World War II. When the war ended, they were released, but homeless and without possessions so they lived on Skid Row in Los Angeles for five years.

But this is America, the land of possibilities—or at least it was in those days. George graduated from high school and went on to pick up a master's degree in theater at UCLA in 1964. A year later he was at the helm of the *USS Enterprise* boldly going through Space, the final frontier.

Even in those days he was attracted by politics. By 1972 he was an alternate delegate to the Democratic National Convention. The next year he ran for Los Angeles City Council and came in second. LA mayor Tom Bradley noticed, and appointed George to the board of directors for the Southern California Rapid Transit District. Billions of dollars changed hands, and he didn't take any of it. So maybe he really wasn't cut out for public office.

Even though George understood his sexual orientation early on, discrimination kept him from acknowledging it to the outside world. In 2005 (at 68 years old) he came out when legislation for same sex marriage began to make notable progress. This further spurred him on to advocate for LGBTQ+ rights. He went on speaking tours and wrote a memoir "They Called Us Enemy," which highlights the challenges he faced in his personal life as a gay man, inspiring many to embrace their authentic selves.

Over the years George's public service announcements championing LGBTQ+, diversity, equity and inclusion issues earned several sharp responses from Donald Trump.

But George was not always outspoken and serious. His many years of postings on have earned him millions of followers due to his humorous postings on science fiction and political satire. "We have what I call a Klingon in the White House," George said. "This authoritarian, self-important, singularly minded person there advocating for erasure."

Meiselas Brothers

17.7 million
@meidastouch.com

Ben, Brett and Jordan Meiselas created MeidasTouch in 2020 and made it into a full-fledged news network.

The Meiselas Brothers brought a new attitude into Democratic politics. Many of the small pieces of new networks now became clear. These are a growing aspect of the Democratic world.

Ben Meiselas became the visible face of the *MeidasTouch Network* and took full advantage of the professional presence he created as the successful attorney for Colin Kaepernick, the kneeling football player. Ben defended Colin from attacks by Donald Trump from 2016 onward. In 2020 he shifted gears to defending democracy from Trump, along with his two talented brothers.

His brother, Brett, is the video artist among them, having won two Emmy Awards for his work on *The Ellen DeGeneres Show*. And in fact their high quality videos helped get *MeidasTouch* off the ground.

Jordan is the marketing expert among the trio, and his savvy contributed to the brothers' success at turning some of their videos into potent ads that affected political outcomes across the country.

That all started in 2020 with the political action committee they formed using this name, with the purpose of preventing Trump's re-election that year. With that mission accomplished, they got into the critical U.S. Senate elections in Georgia, for Raphael Warnock and Jon Ossoff, helping both of them to victory. That gave the Senate a 50-50 split, and allowed Vice-President Kamala Harris to cast the deciding vote on close issues.

MeidasTouch was spun off from the political action committee in 2023, and has been a roaring success ever since. With video being a huge part of what they do, it is no surprise that a major part of their following is on YouTube and TikTok, allowing them to reach many people outside the Old School media of Facebook and X/Twitter. That puts them on the leading edge of bringing people on board the Blue political bandwagon.

MeidasTouch is now bigger than Joe Rogan's podcast.[13] These "pro-democracy warriors" have made it their mission to fact check the continual string a misinformation spewing from Trump and his administration. That is an almost insurmountable task!

Chapter

Six

Good Trouble

Too many of the agonizing stories we hear of people in America having their rights trampled and their financial lives turned upside-down are followed by Democratic officials offering several words of complaint, then going back to the office for "business as usual".

Among the few who have been ongoing examples of highly visible defiance of Trump have been Bernie Sanders and AOC. Their nationwide campaign in 2025 not only went to safe Blue states to complain about Trump's wrong-doings, it went to swing states such as Arizona, Wisconsin and Michigan.

The turn-out of people they attracted in Denver was a massive 34,000. Then that was exceeded in Los Angeles 22 days later. People were fired up and ready to *do* something.

Meanwhile, Republicans were being booed at their own community meetings for supporting Trump's horrid policies. Republican House Speaker Mike Johnson even advised his fellow GOP members not to hold any more of those town hall meetings. That is how low their support had fallen among their own voters![14]

Showing the spirit we wish more people would reflect, local Democrats specifically targeted districts of at-risk Republican Congressmen for not speaking up.

That shows "good trouble" at all levels of the country. But what about the individuals being trampled by Trump? Who was standing up for them?

Susan Crawford, the Wisconsin justice we met earlier, was one of the individuals standing up for regular people like us. And that opened doors for her when a state Supreme Court seat became vacant. The rich-versus-poor divide in this race was exposed when Elon Musk took a major role in the contest. This was the most expensive judicial race in history, with $100 million spent by the two sides. About $25 million was contributed by Musk in his attempt to defeat Crawford.

That gave her opponent $54 million compared to Crawford's $46 million.[15] She drew sympathy and some money from George Soros and J.B. Pritzker, but their combined contribution amounted to less than 15% of Musk's donation. The rest had to be made up from small contributions, and that is where Crawford excelled.

She also had strong positions on the issues the court was going to handle. That agenda included voting rights, abortion laws, worker's protections and political redistricting. Crawford was able to show she stood with the people of the state on those matters, and against Musk's "benefit the wealthy."

Unfortunately there was no direct measure of the number of people who did not vote in the previous national election. But it showed up anyway. Voter turn-out had been neck-and-neck between Democrats and Republicans with Trump winning in 2024. But Crawford won by a 10% margin in 2025.

She faced stiff challenges and prevailed. This is definitely the kind of campaign Democrats need to be running this year.

Several other Democratic leaders have also been going out and causing good trouble, such as Senator Chris Van Hollen of Maryland.

When one of his constituents, Kilmar Abrego Garcia, was illegally deported to El Salvador's maximum security prison, the case was taken all the way to the Supreme Court. The court ruled Trump and his administration needed to facilitate Garcia's return to the USA.

Trump turned his back on the court, with his Attorney General saying Garcia was not coming back. His Homeland Security Secretary, Kristi Noem, went further and told Congress Garcia was *never* coming back.

That should have been a constitutional crisis, with the Supreme Court insisting that its ruling be followed. But that would have required a Supreme Court with enough integrity and backbone to stand up to Trump. And that is not *this* Supreme Court.

Fortunately Senator Van Hollen had all the strength-of-character needed. He flew to El Salvador and insisted upon seeing Garcia. Eventually the meeting was held, confirming that Garcia was still alive and available to be returned. An outraged Trump called Van Hollen a fool and a grandstander. But eventually Garcia was brought back to the U.S.

Van Hollen showed it is definitely possible to stand up to Trump and get him to back down.

Democratic leadership needs to take a lesson from Senator Van Hollen and show that *action* is the name of this game.

Chapter

Seven

Getting Involved

The Resistance is doing some remarkable things these days. Protest rallies of 8 million people are showing up nationwide. Special elections are pressing forward to much-needed wins. The internet is being flooding with news ignored or downplayed by traditional media. The election playing field is being reshaped for critical 2026 and 2028 elections. If these sound like the kinds of things you'd like to be part of, that's easy to do.

Just get on social media and start following the 20 Resistance leaders being highlighted here. Of course, there are many other good people there as well, but this is an essential starter list.

Immediately you will begin hearing about things that are not covered in the news. Mistakes by the administration are highlighted rather than covered up. Upcoming rallies are announced ahead of time, in case one of them hits a subject near and dear to your heart. The Resistance custom now is to have simultaneous rallies in every state, so there is probably a location near you, where you can go and be with people who are fired up about the same thing that gets you going.

One thing to consider is that different social media have different levels of Resistance involvement. Facebook and X/Twitter are the old-time standards, and many people are still there. Instagram and TikTok are new and highly visual, if that works for you. YouTube is halfway between those two camps, as a familiar visual medium. But the most steadily-Resistance-oriented media is Bluesky. It's very much like X/Twitter but without all the MAGA trolls and Elon Musk tributes.

The bottom line is that you have choices. There's no cost to sign up for participation, and one of these is likely to be a great fit for you.

Once the stream of the Resistance is flowing to your screen, you can decide which avenues you'd like to follow the most. Even just keeping yourself informed is already helping the cause!

But what if you want to go farther? We are all being hurt by what Trump is doing in one way or another. Sometimes in several ways. But what can you do about it? Complain to a neighbor, family member or bartender?

That may give a little relief, but what does it accomplish? How about if you could complain and offer suggestions to people who are working hard to kick Trump's rear end and would really appreciate having you around?

If the last choice sounds good to you, consider posting your opinions online where other Resisters can see them.

You probably know things can go viral on social media, and it's amazing to see that happen. How would you like to be *making* it happen?

It's much easier to make things go viral when you're talking about saving the country from Donald Trump. Millions of people are on board with that idea. If you come up with a meme, gif, picture or a few good words, people will like, comment and repost it. If it strikes enough people the right way, it's "viral city". And wow does that feel great!

Those of us who have been in the Resistance a long time recognize that all our good ideas come from other people in the Resistance. That could include you.

We basically crowd-sourced everything in this book. Reading the comments and suggestions from many members of the Resistance leads to some form of consensus on ways forward. And goal number one has been to be to get as many mad-at-Trump people together as possible. Then take whatever actions we agree upon—such as rallies attended by millions of people nationwide.

So speak up. You can be an important part of making all of this work!

One of the things you'll find here is so many really good people who want the same thing you do.

In fact, that is how all of this came about. We've been reading your posts, replies, and seeing what goes viral on your pages. If you've been online at Facebook, X/Twitter, Bluesky, Instagram, YouTube or wherever, you've influenced us to some degree.

These are not the recommendations we would have crowd-sourced a year or two ago. The level of anger at the mess coming out of Washington, DC is higher now. The level of disappointment with some Democratic leadership is greater now. The avenues for going forward feel completely different these days.

And of course that does not mean everyone agrees on everything. We don't have someone in a silly red hat telling us what to do. But most of the things you see here will give you a warm and fuzzy feeling because this really *is* how we feel about things right now. Details are worked out on the spot as events unfold.

You can be part of all that, to whatever extent you like. There are lots of ways to impact things for the better. So find yours and do it!

Democratic
Influencers
9 thru 12

George Conway, Allison Gill, JoJoFromJerz & Aaron Rupar

George Conway

3.2 million
@gtconway
Once married to Kellyanne Conway (Trump's 2016 campaign manager), he is now rabidly anti-Trump.

Although his early years found him at the conservative end of the spectrum, George's love of democracy and opposition to Trump set him on a more balanced path.

In the 1990's George was one of the attorneys representing Paula Jones in her sexual harassment lawsuit against Bill Clinton. Anne Coulter and Matt Drudge were part of the team. He was also dating Laura Ingraham at the time. So he was swimming in fairly conservative waters.

Apparently it was Anne who introduced him to Kellyanne, and they were married in 2001. Sixteen years later Kellyanne was managing Trump's successful campaign, and George was in line for a cushy appointment in Washington, DC.

But he just couldn't get over his doubts about Trump. Those doubts deepened and by 2018 he was publicly challenging Trump's positions and actions.[16]

The next year George joined with other long-time Republicans to start the Lincoln Project dedicated to defeating Trump in 2020. Clearly this caused problems at home, and by 2023 he and Kellyanne were divorced.

As his experiences show, the coalition of people in America who want Trump out now embraces a wide range of individuals on the political spectrum.

The trick will be to get everyone to vote on election day. George and others like him can help people with conservative leanings walk across that bridge to our side, and pull their ballot into the right box.

Allison Gill

1.7 million

@muellershewrote.com

Allison Gill hosts the "Mueller, She Wrote" podcast and owns the media company sponsoring the show.

Allison was fired by the Trump administration from her job at the Veterans Administration in apparent retaliation for producing a left-leaning podcast.

That podcast was her fabulously popular *Mueller, She Wrote.* Allison had started it in 2017 with a couple of friends when Robert Mueller was appointed as special counsel to investigate any connection between the Trump campaign and Russia the previous year. She deftly separated real news from political double-speak, and did it with a bit of humor.

As a veteran herself, Allison was attracted to the VA many years earlier to help other vets. And she had gradually worked her way up to a significantly responsible position. Given all of that, she had been very careful in her podcast to only go by the name "A.G." and keep it completely separate from her work, as required by law for government employees.

But since her podcast did not toe the Trump line, it apparently rubbed some loyalists the wrong way.

When she was assigned to a new supervisor in 2019, he promptly took steps to relocate her job and to investigate her podcast, obviously trying to get her to quit.[17] When she refused to leave, she was terminated.

But just like an older generation had their "Unsinkable Molly Brown," we have Allison. She has continued to expand her resistance work with her *The Breakdown* newsletter as well as *Daily Beans* and *Cleanup on Aisle 45* podcasts. And she now owns MSW Media which supports these efforts and more.

Go, lassie, go.

JoJoFromJerz

2.4 million
@jojofromjerz

Joanne Carducci is best known as JoJoFromJerz, the housemom who became a snarky internet sensation.

JoJoFromJerz is intriguing. You would never guess she is also Joanne Carducci, the mom of two kids in a suburban house 45 miles west of New York City. She still looks like the blond "it" girl at your high school that all the guys were crazy about. But one with a very definite opinion about where Trump should stick his next executive order.

One can easily imagine her walking past Tony Soprano's table in an Italian restaurant and saying, "What are *you* looking at?"

Some out-of-country background actually fits her, because Jo grew up in her New Jersey home with a father who was originally from Lebanon. His opinions were as far to the right as hers were to the left, so she learned at an early age to fearlessly stand her ground.

But all of the plans she had at college to change the world somehow were overcome by life's small adventures. The next thing she knew, many years had passed and she was caring for her two kids, a difficult marital relationship and a house in the suburbs. She still has the kids and the house.

And she gained a purpose in life in the form of a natural disaster. In 2016 it rode down an escalator under a mop of orange hair and announced it was running for president. Trump was already branding immigrants as criminals, and maybe the insult splashed a little mud on her father. In any event, she definitely wanted to straighten out the escalator guy.

In her Red neighborhood, saying anything would not have been a good idea. So she went on Twitter and did it there. And people cheered her on. So she did it again.

After Trump was kicked out and Joe Biden became president, Jo Carducci shared a special moment at the White House with my wife and I. It was magical. Jo was the one who captured the photo as I spoke to the president about my immigrant grandfather and how proud he would've been of what we were doing.

When it was Jo's turn to talk with Biden, she shared her own thoughts of her immigrant dad who had such an impact on her life. And the president hung on every word.

All these years later, Jo is still saying the things online that people would love to say but can't find the words. She can find the words. Which is easy for her because some of them are only four letters long.

JoJoFromJerz. A force of nature!

Aaron Rupar

2.3 million
@atrupar

An independent journalist covering US politics, he publishes the Public Notice newsletter.

Aaron is one of the people bringing the heartland of America into the circle of Blue influencers. Born and raised in Minnesota, he decided to take his journalism work to Washington, DC, where the action was.

Arriving on Super Tuesday in 2016 when so many presidential primary elections were being held, he went independent for a while. Two years later he decided to go to work for *VOX*, the news and opinion site noted for its explanatory journalism.

The digital age allowed him to combine both worlds, returning to Minnesota while working online with *VOX*.

But the desire to go independent again finally became to much to bear in 2021. So he left *VOX* and launched his Public Notice newsletter on Substack. That rocket went straight up, and he has been enjoying strongly-growing readership ever since.

Aaron has also found the time to co-host the weekly *Nir & Rupar* podcast with David Nir, known for his *Downballot* coverage of election races.

Always something new!

Chapter

Eight

How Bad Is It?

If you are reading national news, you may not realize how mad you really should be. The legacy TV and cable channels, newspapers and magazines are so afraid of Trump, or adoring of Trump, that major events are being watered down or even ignored. It's not until you tap into the Resistance that you find out how perilously difficult things really are.

We're talking about videos from people who attend press conferences, verified news sourced from Associated Press foreign affiliates, and international publications such as The Guardian.

You can't be any more accurate about what Trump and his underlings are saying than that.

As one of the Resistance journalists and commentators who attend press conferences whenever possible, I know the magic that comes with hearing words directly from people's mouths, and seeing it played back on video. During the Biden years, we had great access to record these events, and even to talk one-on-one with the speakers afterward—on the record!

As you can imagine, during the Trump years that has dried up almost completely. In a free and open society, press credentials are issued to all media. I'll leave it to you to conclude what kind of society we live in under Trump.

But a shout-out is due here to Acyn Torabi. He dedicates himself 24 hours a day (it seems) to capturing every video clip related to the news from every available source and making it available to repost with added commentary. So if you're ever wondering, "Did they really say that?" Acyn knows. And has it on video!

I just love putting truth and facts right back in the face of Donald Trump and his crew!

One of the other sources deserving of some attention is Really American. It was born out of frustration with so much of the political media being detached from the urgency of the moment. Built as a digital-first platform, it set out to meet audiences where they already were, on social feeds, in short videos, and inside the fast-moving current of online conversation.

From the start, Really American focused on rapid-response content. When political flashpoints erupt, the outlet moves quickly, producing clips, commentary, and shareable videos designed to shape the narrative in real time. Its tone is unapologetic and values-driven, positioning itself as openly pro-democracy and willing to challenge extremism directly.

Someone else who has not been afraid to speak up and say what's real is Senator Chris Murphy from Connecticut. He deserves credit for ripping open the little shop of horrors Secretary of Homeland Security Kristi Noem was running with ICE and the rest of her domain. This was how he unloaded on her in a Congressional meeting during May of 2025.

> "I say this with seriousness and respect, but your department is out of control. You are spending like you don't have a budget. You are on the verge of running out of money for the fiscal year. You are illegally refusing to spend funds that have been authorized by this Congress and appropriated by this committee. You are ignoring the immigration laws of this nation,

implementing a brand-new immigration system that you have invented that has little relation to the statutes that you are required – that you are commanded – to follow as spelled out in your oath of office. You are routinely violating the rights of immigrants who may not be citizens, but whether you like it or not, have constitutional and statutory rights when they reside in the United States. Your agency acts as if laws don't matter, as if the election gave you some mandate to violate the Constitution and the laws passed by this Congress. It did not give you that mandate. You act as if your disagreement with the law – or even the public's disagreement with the law – is relevant and gives you the ability to create your own law. It does not give you that ability.

"… this obsession with spending at the border, as the Chairwoman mentioned, has left the country unprotected elsewhere. The security threats to the United States are higher, not lower, than before Trump came to office. To fund the border, you have illegally gutted spending for cybersecurity. As we speak, Russian and Chinese hackers are having a field day

> attacking our nation. You have withdrawn funds for disaster prevention. Storms are going to kill more people in this country because of your illegal withholding of these funds. Your myopia about the border, fueled by President Trump's prejudice against people who speak a different language, has shattered many of this country's most important defenses."[18]
>
> *Senator Chris Murphy*
> *May 8, 2025*

If you will allow me to repeat the earlier point, no matter how irritated you are about what Trump is doing, the more you find out, the madder you're going to be. And justifiably so. Following Resisters on social media is the easiest way to find out what is really happening.

Chapter

Nine

No Kings

Expressing opinions and exposing Trump's bad deeds are great things to do. But when you really get angry, show up in person. You'll have lots of company because there are a whole lot of upset people in the US lately, in the wake of Trump, Musk and other characters leading a march of destruction from sea to sea.

Showing up at protest rallies has been raised to an art form by members of the Resistance. Again, credit to the people at 50501, because having rallies in all 50 states at the same time has allowed millions of people to participate, be seen, and be heard.

As mentioned, a particularly spectacular "Hands Off" rally was held on April 5 of 2025 with about four million people showing up from coast to coast. The largest demonstrations on that day were at state capitals, where TV cameras were gathered. Many other demonstrations were scattered across each state.

At the Phoenix suburb of Tempe in critical swing-state Arizona a local rally consisted of perhaps a thousand people. There were older folks with gray hair and hats to protect against the sun, wearing solid-color loose clothing and the occasional tie-dyed shirt. Middle-aged folks sported sunglasses, shorts and t-shirts stenciled with imaginative slogans such as "Self-respecting women don't vote for rapists." Teenage-to-twenty-somethings were campaigning in faded Levi's and comfortable shirts.

Those cheerful warriors packed themselves onto the long pedestrian overpass above the 60 Freeway with handmade protest signs. During the protest about 50,000 people drove under that bridge. The forest of placards assembled there ran the gamut from "A Woman's Place Is in the Revolution" to "The Constitution Is Not a Suggestion!" to "Fight Truth Decay" to "I've Seen Better Cabinets at Ikea."

Some of us on the bridge were old enough to remember Freedom Marches and Vietnam War protests. Younger folks were seeing people rise up for the first time, their eyes wide in fascination.

It was a moment. On that mild, sunny, springtime day, it was the place to be.

More rallies followed, grouped under the "No Kings" name. And more people showed up each time, building up to the eight-million people size.

It should be mentioned that in addition to these mega-rallies, many people still rallied for specific causes which were near and dear to their heart. These were either at the same time as the huge rallies or on their own chosen days. No issue was forgotten. Even anti-Tesla rallies happened. That didn't use to be a thing, but with Elon Musk's horrible track record, it took on a certain popularity.

People have been showing up in other ways too. Some Resisters enjoy the well-established path of meeting in small groups with other active people and figuring out local actions they can take, as well a jumping in on the national events.

Others regularly attend Zoom or other online meetings with large numbers of people enthusiastic about doing some particular things to right Trump's wrongs. We will look inside many of those groups in just a minute.

But one of the best ways to reach people has been where they already are: online. For years, Republicans understood something it appeared Democratic lawmakers and their consultants didn't: influence moves through culture. Republicans weren't just campaigning—they were showing up on podcasts, YouTube channels, and social feeds, shaping everyday conversations long before Democrats realized that's where the country was listening. They built a formidable content machine that looked like news but functioned as propaganda. Right-Wing personalities were given institutional credibility and support—flying on Air force One and appearing on stages next to Donald Trump. That was the gap Democratic influencers have been struggling to fill.

In 2017 the idea of interviewing a member of Congress felt impossible. Then came 2024. Washington's post-election autopsy confirmed what many of us already knew: the Left didn't just need better messaging. It needed the infrastructure to amplify it.

And that's when everything changed. Washington realized that platforms like *Call to Activism, MeidasTouch* and *Mueller, She Wrote* already had built-in audiences--communities ready to listen, share, and mobilize. Overnight, the dynamic flipped. Lawmakers who once overlooked digital creators began reaching out and wanting to collaborate, come on our shows, and speak directly to the audiences we'd built.

Today, members of Congress and other leaders seek us out because our platforms are not just reaching people, they are mobilizing them.

Drawing from direct experience, my interviews are averaging around one million views, in a network that reaches six million followers. This generates a weekly 115 million views on X, Facebook and Instagram and six billion views annually across all platforms. That scale means lawmakers aren't just appearing in the echo-chamber of mainstream news. They are bypassing filters and speaking directly to the people paying attention. They are clarifying, pushing back and humanizing, without waiting for a sound bite to hopefully make the evening news.

Even late-night hosts like Jimmy Kimmel have reportedly been warned by FCC officials about "crossing lines." If comedians face that kind of pressure over punchlines, imagine what reporters endure when their corporate owners are chasing a merger and need to stay on the FCC's good side.

That's why platforms such as *Call to Activism, MeidasTouch* and *Mueller, She Wrote* exist—to tell the truth with purpose, not permission. To say what others can't, and to remind people that a free press doesn't just live in newsrooms or on cable anymore. It lives wherever citizens raise their voices to defend democracy. We just have to show up to make it happen.

Because in the end, it's not about the numbers. It's about impact. Its about truth. And about never forgetting that all our voices together can make a movement.

Democratic
Influencers
13 thru 16

Marc Elias,
Heather Cox Richardson,
BrooklynDad_Defiant!
& Jim Acosta

Marc Elias

2.8 million
@marcelias
The master litigation attorney who defeated all 64 of Trump's "Stop the Steal" lawsuits nationwide.

Marc arrived in Washington, DC, in 1993 with the ink still wet on his Duke law degree. He found Newt Gingrich employing a successful tactic of filing lawsuits against Democratic candidates to affect the outcome of elections. Marc admits that he was "young, cheap, aggressive, and interested in criminal law"—enough so to take on the work of defending against those attacks.[19]

As a result he soon he found himself at the prestigious Perkins Coie law firm with a fast-growing reputation in the field of political law. He served as general counsel for the presidential campaign of John Kerry in 2004, then had a similar role for Al Franken's U.S. Senate election in 2008.

Eight years later he was general counsel for Hillary Clinton's presidential campaign against Trump. During that campaign Elias hired a consultant to look into Trump's possible ties to Russia. The resulting report not only proved unreliable, it was apparently charged to the Clinton campaign without its knowledge. A difficult time.

But 2020 brought a long string of victories. Marc was charged with countering Trump's "Stop the

Steal" campaign, and won victories in all 64 of those court cases.

That seemed an appropriate time to shift gears, so he started his own legal practice and left Perkins Coie. Along with that he created the *Democracy Docket* website which is now the go-to source for anything having to do with voting rights and elections litigation.

In 2024 Marc was back in his familiar role as general counsel for a presidential campaign, this time for Kamala Harris. With voting rights still under attack, he will probably be quite busy for the foreseeable future.

Heather Cox Richardson

9.2 million
@hcrichardson

She teaches history at Boston College, and her Letters from an American are often #1 on Substack.

Having been at Harvard for her whole undergraduate and graduate life, Heather Cox Richardson knows better than most people the pain her alma mater is going through at the hands of Donald Trump.

He loathes anyone who stands up for truth and reality, as Harvard has done. And as Heather has done every day since 2019 with her *Letters from an American*. And it was an inspired idea.

Each night—or sometimes in the early morning haze—she writes a letter about the notable events of the day in the context of American history. Each of them also keeps an eye on what that means for American democracy.

As you can imagine, with Trump constantly stirring up a storm, she never lacks for material.

Although Facebook was her original home, her letters seem better suited to Substack, where they currently reside. And since it's possible to subscribe for free, that works well all the way around.

BrooklynDad_Defiant!

2.0 million

@mmpadellan

M.M. Padellan, better known as BrooklynDad_Defiant! is a New York art director when not online.

The first thing you notice about Majid M. Padellan is his fiery spirit. If you thought all art directors were soft-spoken, artistic types—think again. Majid is the explosive artistic type. And when the subject is (an orange-haired) man's inhumanity to man, he really gets going.

Maybe that comes from having lived life close to the edge. In the 1990s he had fallen under the influence of drugs and hit a super low. He lost his family, his work and his place to live. Out on the street he met a doorman on Christmas Eve who prayed with him and got him to try one more time to work his stuff out. For some unknown reason, it worked. He got out.

That was more than twenty years ago. Never touched it again. Clean the whole time. New family. New job, working for himself. Mindful of helping other people. Has to be, after what others did for him.

And he really doesn't take B.S. of any kind. You hear it when he talks. You see it when he writes.

Why would people listen to this guy? Why would they not? He has lived more than most of us, and makes the world seem a little more real when he's there.

People seem to like that.

Throw in a truly artistic mind and you get an artist who can bring political pictures to life. That is what happened in his full-color illustrated book *The Liddle'est President*. It showed Trump as a spoiled child in the White House. And people loved it.

When Biden was president, I always enjoyed running into Majid at White House events. We would huddle and discuss how to best communicate important issues. What stood out wasn't just his passion, it was his strategic mind. That combination of heart and strategy makes him a rare force in this fight. I'm glad he's on our side.

Jim Acosta

3.6 million
@jimacosta
As CNN's news anchor he clashed with Trump, was demoted and quit, showing great personal courage.

Born and raised in Virginia, Jim's first job after graduating with a degree in communications was at a radio station in Washington, DC.

The world opened up in 1995 when he moved in front of a TV camera by accepting the job as a news reporter at the NBC affiliate in Knoxville, Tennessee.

The camera liked him, but he then began what essentially was a tour of America. He had to keep moving to earn ever-increasing responsibilities. Fort Worth, Chicago, New York City and Atlanta saw him delivering the news.

Finally he landed at CNN in 2007, which would be his home for the next eighteen years. He covered the Democratic campaigns of Barack Obama and Hillary Clinton the next year, and eventually became the network's chief White House correspondent.

His clashes with Trump became legendary, leading up to a grand face-off on November 7, 2018. At a White House press conference Jim tried to ask a follow-up question, but Trump started talking to another reporter. There were voices all talking over each other.

Afterwards Jim's White House press credentials were taken away, using the excuse that he had pushed away the arm of an intern who was trying to take his microphone away. Apparently doctored footage was provided to "prove" the point.

So CNN sued to get Jim's access restored and it became national news. After beating each other up in court, a compromise was reached giving Jim access again, but limiting him to one question only unless given permission for another.

When Trump started his second term, CNN apparently decided discretion was the better part of valor and shunted Jim to a different assignment. He would have none of it, and quit.

Following the example of other Blue influencers Jim now works for himself, hosting *The Jim Acosta Show* on Substack and YouTube.

Chapter

Ten

Indivisible, 50501 & Democratic Clubs

Every once in a while, I enjoy sitting in on a Zoom session with Indivisible founders Leah Greenberg and Ezra Levin. They are always into whatever is happening right then, and still seem to have the same enthusiasm as they did years ago. It's also a great perk for members of Indivisible who not only get their local-meeting impact but also the big picture as seen from a high level.

These days much of that higher level is in close connection with 50501. Started by many activists, this new group's first event was an anti-Trump rally on February 5, 2025. That was followed by the major

"Hands Off" rally on April 5, 2025. Then "No King's Day" on June 14. Several more No King's Days followed. These beautiful expressions of patriotism and love of democracy added a much-needed positive air to the public discussion of what was happening.

Democratic clubs used to be the most commonly seen manifestation of left-wing political activity in America. They are still one of the most reliable sources of pro-democracy action. But their number has been beaten down over the years. My own club was forced to merge with another one years ago to stay afloat. We're all going through a period of change right now.

Years ago, many clubs clogged the Westside of Los Angeles. They stretched from West Hollywood to Beverly Hills, Westwood (UCLA), Brentwood, Santa Monica and the surrounding area. We opened a Westside campaign office every two years on a main street. A flyer called "The Westside Story" was printed and inserted in every club's monthly bulletin across the area. Now the clubs have become only a shadow of what they were before.

Some people fearlessly keep the old Democratic club fires burning. Others are now trying newer offerings with online components. Some have just been staying home. But this may be a good time to look around and find a good Democratic home away from home.

Many other groups across the country have also been contributing to the defense of democracy these days. These include the Sierra Club, Occupy Wall Street, Move On, NAACP, Progressive Democrats, Democratic Socialists and a long list of others.

Remember, we're all stronger together!

One of the biggest contributions to the growth of Democratic clubs in recent years has been the explosion of special elections, primary elections and preparations for general elections. It has been showing us that we really do have power at the ballot box when we choose to use it.

At a New Jersey special election on April 16, 2026, Analilia Mejia won a seat in Congress. Even though she was running for the first time, Analilia connected with local voters and did all the right things so that when the polls closed at 8:00, she was pronounced the winner at 8:07 by Associated Press.

To give an idea of what she accomplished, Analilia was filling the vacancy left by Mikie Sherrill, who was so popular that she was elected governor of New Jersey. Two years earlier Mikie had won this congressional seat by 15%. Analilia won it by an astounding 26%.

Voters were really mad at Trump, and she made the most of it. A good lesson for us all.

For two hundred and fifty years local clubs and groups have continued the work of the American

Revolution in every city and sizable town. Over those years their leaders included Benjamin Franklin, Samuel Adams, George Washington, Thomas Jefferson, James Madison, Alexander Hamilton and many others.

Those early leaders were rallied by a powerful handbook called "Common Sense" composed by Thomas Paine. Recorded on only 47 pages in 1775, this small masterpiece was finally published on January 10, 1776. Its concise and compelling words rallied all the pro-revolution people scattered across the thirteen states and gave them common cause to work together and create a new country.

Then the Declaration of Independence fired up the land again on July 4, 1776. In only 1320 words it raised people's spirits with unforgettable words such as:

"We hold these truths to be self-evident, that all men are created equal, that they are endowed by their Creator with certain unalienable Rights, that among these are Life, Liberty and the pursuit of Happiness."

Another short document, the Constitution of the United States became the law of the land on March 4 of 1789. It has stayed in effect until Donald Trump began to take it apart in 2025. It inspired us with:

"WE THE PEOPLE of the United States, in Order to form a more perfect Union, establish Justice, insure domestic Tranquility, provide for the common defense, promote the general Welfare, and secure the Blessings of Liberty to ourselves and our Posterity, do ordain and establish this Constitution for the United States of America."

This tradition of short works that inspire continued in 2017 with "On Tyranny" by Timothy Snyder, protesting what Donold Trump was doing to our country. It offered gems of wisdom such as: "Do not obey in advance" which have now become widely repeated in America.

Imagine your civil rights being curtailed, military troops massing at the border, and your family finances ruined by tariffs and price increases. This could be you in today's America. Or it could have been you in the 1770s American colonies, being pushed into a desperate revolt.

In those ancient days when Ben Franklin and Paul Revere walked cobblestone streets, people still gathered at the famous Liberty Tree near Boston Common to find out what they could do about the oppressive Redcoats.

In today's America people come together in person and on social media to find out what they can do about the oppressive Redhats.

And as we are seeing, there is much to be done.

Chapter

Eleven

Influencing Others

Expanding your impact on elections becomes easier by influencing other people on social media. Just by participating you're having a noticeable effect on local or national campaigns. Your "likes" on other people's posts encourages those individuals to do more. That's influence. Joining with other people to stack up on a post lets people know this is important—so people take it more seriously.

Then when you and others go to the next level and jump on something so it goes viral, that can seriously change how people think and act. The thing is *hot,* so people adjust accordingly.

When you become good at that and use it to push back on Trump or the candidates he favors, then you become a participant of considerable value.

Here is what you can do even if you are fairly new to social media. And then a look at what you can do if you're more experienced and choose to increase your impact.

Not much involved on social media yet?

The time-honored way to get rolling is to just follow other people who have similar interests to your own. The more you follow, the more people will naturally follow you back. But it's not just a numbers game. If these really are people who share your interest in a particular candidate or cause, they are highly motivated to add a comment in response. And they may even re-post your opinion so that it has a chance to start going viral.

But the most important thing to do, if you want more people to respect what you have to say, and be influenced by it, is to stay active. Enjoy the interaction with people. It's long distance, it's safe, and you don't even have to put on a clean shirt to do it.

Just post your material, re-post good material by other people, comment, like, and give a shout-out to friends once in a while. People who share your interests get attracted by all that. It multiplies your following, and multiplies the responses to the opinions you post.

What could be better than that?

Already active on social media and political issues?

If you are already active and have a decent number of people reading your opinions and observations, there are numerous ways to step that up and have your posts draw many more likes, comments and reposts. Oddly enough, one of the best is quite similar to the way you got started on social media—just by shining some light on people who agree with you and enabling *them* to grow and be heard.

For example, when my wife Cosima and I interviewed House Oversight Committee member Robert Garcia on November 12, 2025, we learned more Epstein emails were coming. So first that got published to all our readers. Then I re-posted comments by seven of our loyal readers, giving each of them exposure to our entire base of readers.

That is why this Epstein post had 2,900 reposts and 10,000 likes.

In similar manner I was able to turn House Speaker Mike Johnson's words against him about that same time, and share the attention with others, resulting in 14,000 reposts and 109,000 likes.

Sharing good things with other people can also reflect well on you.

The slogan "Stronger together" isn't just a saying in this world, it's a visible reality.

A lesser-known secret

There is, however, one huge secret known to people who have hundreds of thousands of followers. It's a thing called Substack.

Substack is a site where anyone can post any blog article they want to write. And they get to earn money by doing it, in addition to the modest fame and quickly-growing followers.

The trick is, they have to post regularly. The big players pick some pattern, such as four days of guaranteed publication, plus an article on one of the other three days.

One easy way they generate new material all the time is to interview people. Anyone with a little expertise on something in the news is a good choice. People like to listen to someone with inside info, and a slant they haven't already heard in the news. Those things are also nice because videoclips are an easy spin-off and can be posted on YouTube or other places, even it you don't have a big presence there.

Best of all, anyone can sign up to read your articles for free on Substack. And that is the right price for getting lots of followers. Then those subscribers, as they are called, are invited to become paid subscribers and enjoy additional benefits. Those benefits can include an occasional session with a major influencer that's limited to paid subscribers. Or it includes the ability to ask questions of a major influencer and get an answer.

Once you go onto Substack, it does wonders for your self-esteem to be circulating with the big boys and girls.

And to tell you the truth, there needs to be more of this kind of thing. There have to be ways major influencers can get at least some compensation for all the work they do, and for all the times they lift us up when we really need a boost. Not only that, they are trailblazers. And they are one of our strongest lines of defense against the load of garbage rolling downhill these days from Washington, DC.

Democratic Influencers 17 thru 20

Robert Reich, Don Lemon, Aaron Parnas & Fred Wellman

Robert Reich

13.2 million
@rbreich

Professor of public policy at UC Berkeley who served in the Cabinet of his friend Bill Clinton.

A formative moment in Robert's life happened when he was graduating from a New York high school and a classmate was murdered in Mississippi for registering Black voters. That was 1964 and he has been a devoted Democrat ever since, even venturing into Progressive territory.

At Dartmouth Robert dated Hillary Rodham, but eventually lost out to another friend of his, Bill Clinton. At Yale Law School he was a classmate of Bill, Hillary and Clarence Thomas . Strange bedfellows, so to speak.

Robert was teaching at Harvard when Bill Clinton was elected president in 1992, and promptly accepted the position of Secretary of Labor in his cabinet. He had great influence as a Friend of Bill. And in the sometimes backstabbing days of Washington, DC, he credited Hillary with keeping him informed of what was afoot.[20]

In 2006 Robert became a professor at UC Berkeley's Goldman School of Public Policy and is still active there.

In 2015 He and Jacob Kornbluth started Inequality Media which produces current-events videos including *The Common Good* on YouTube, where he has 1.2 million subscribers.

And he is still a friend of Bill's.

Don Lemon

8.3 million
@donlemonofficial
A former CNN star, Don is now a commentator making waves on his own.

One of the most outspoken journalists in America, Don Lemon has held important positions at NBC and CNN. Unfortunately that trait also brought his long career at CNN to an end when he was accused of being misogynistic. His outspoken nature has made him susceptible to such characterizations for various reasons.

His challenging of statements by Donald Trump since 2018 has also opened a testy relationship between him and supporters of the "supreme leader". When he was fired from CNN, Lemon landed an interview with Elon Musk. But after the questions had been asked, that broadcast was cancelled due to its aggressive nature.

Even into 2026, Lemon was a journalist investigating the federal Metro Surge operations in Minnesota when he was arrested on charges from the U.S. Department of Justice. This brought strong objections from freedom-of-speech organizations across the country. Don seems to never be afraid of stirring up controversies.

Aaron Parnas

10.8 million
@aaronparnas

At only 27 years of age, Aaron is already a major presence online, active on many platforms.

Now one of the leading Gen Z voices, Aaron is shaping how news is consumed today. An independent journalist, commentator, strategist, and attorney, Aaron has quickly become a key figure in the national political conversation, offering sharp insights at the intersection of law, media, and policy.

He first gained widespread attention through viral, educational content breaking down complex political issues in a fast, accessible way—particularly resonating with younger, highly engaged audiences. His rapid-response analysis of major court decisions, legislative battles, and election narratives has made him a trusted public voice.

He played a significant role in shaping the digital narrative around the 2022 and 2024 election cycles, with his rapid-response commentary. During Senator Cory Booker's record-breaking 25-hour Senate speech protesting the Trump administration's policies, Aaron conducted the second interview—following Rachel Maddow—highlighting how quickly he's become part of the political conversation.

He graduated from Florida Atlantic University with a B.A. in political science and criminal justice at age 18, and earned his J.D. from The George Washington University Law School at 21—one of the youngest ever to do so.

Fred Wellman

1.5 million
@fpwellman
A decorated Army pilot, he now hosts the On Democracy Channel on YouTube and other podcasts.

If you happen to be a veteran, you couldn't find a better person to keep you plugged into what you really want to know than Fred Wellman.

It's not just that he graduated from West Point, went into service as an Army helicopter pilot and was constantly assigned to war zones in the Middle East. His twenty-two years of duty gradually included public affairs postings helping people understand what the hell was going on—and sometimes it really was hell.

He's the kind of guy you want in your corner in any difficult situation. He's the one who has your back and will level with you about what it takes to get to the other side of a munitions or political minefield.

These days his *On Democracy* podcast is doing that for the Resistance, augmented by his *On the Line with VoteVets*. This guy is the real deal. Find out for yourself.

Chapter

Twelve

Stronger Than Fox News

Fox News has a huge right-wing lead in the American media market over any left-wing opposition such as MSNBC/(**MS NOW)**. The broadcast channels (ABC, CBS, NBC) used to command more attention, but have fallen into the position of supporting the current administration's fake news too often.

With well-known Democratic movers and shakers in broadcast production such as Oprah Winfrey, Mark Cuban, Steven Spielberg and countless others this has a been a ridiculously underdeveloped area. And understandably so. With popular and message-bearing programs of their own such as Saving Private Ryan, Shark Tank and The Color Purple, they had their own guiding star. But now that their country may be drawing its last moments of breath as a democracy, Lady Liberty needs immediate mouth-to-mouth resuscitation to survive.

Hollywood and New York City are the unrivaled world leaders in media production.

But Resistors have much more than that going for them. They have a rich base of content creators who produce an unending flow of analysis, insight, investigation, stunning video, and even a measure of humor to poke fun at Trump gaffes and failures. Many of these content creators are prominent media professionals being forced out by MAGA pressures . . . think Stephen Colbert, Jim Acosta and others.

This is a vast resource of talent, industry know-how, and people-who-know-people.

And that is important because their mountains of talent need to be mentored by Spielberg, Winfrey, et al to be a profitable channel or other media format which spins off entertainment programs by popular artists. A successful channel does not live by news alone, but requires balanced programming to attract viewers to TV sets. These mega stars should be given a free hand in developing possible directions, and go with whatever attracts the most attention.

On the news side, people overwhelmingly want this offering. Trump's approval ratings have been negative even before he began signing his disastrous proclamations. And have fallen lower ever since. A huge majority of Americans want to know what is actually happening in our country because it effects their life and their families.

The wealth of Resistance talent such as George Clooney, Taylor Swift and Denzel Washington creates an environment that brings far more than simple news programming. The possibilities for sheer entertainment and investigative programming are endless.

The Meiselas Brothers have already shown many of the skills needed to develop news programs. They should be one of the go-to sources for programming and ideas. These three brothers have the lead commentator, video and marketing skills to pull together successful programs.

Allison Gill is similarly of creative and entrepreneurial bent, having already created multiple outlets and organizational structures with *Mueller, She Wrote* and similar programs.

In terms of raw talent, Rachel Maddow shows clearly that Resisters can drive a strong news team. In fact she might be interested in developing a longer line of talented individuals and programming.

Jim Acosta is one of the talents just waiting for a major challenge. There is no telling how far he might go.

Leah Greenberg and Ezra Levin have the inside-Washington understanding that could lead directly to Sunday analyst programs or other areas which they may wish to develop.

On that fine line between news and entertainment, don't forget Resisters such as Aaron Rupar, JoJoFromJerz, Joe Gallina and BrooklynDad_Defiant! If you put these four people together in a room you'll get ten new ideas for shows.

Behind them are literally thousands of influencers who are already producing content on a regular basis. Whenever the exploratory team begins to look at talent for the next batch of new superstars, there is a long line of experienced Resistance commentators available.

Chapter

Thirteen

The Endgame

Resisters have been making a difference in special elections all across America. Even in the state of Florida there was an eye-opening moment in their legislative elections. March 25, 2026 saw Democrat Emily Gregory elected in the district that includes Mar-A-Lago, defeating Donald Trump's own endorsed candidate.

She was continuing what has become a long march across the backroads of America.

Do you remember the woman in Oklahoma City who was a U.S. citizen, at home with her three daughters when ICE broke down her front door, shamed her kids, and took everyone's cell phones and money?

If you thought that kind of blatant mistreatment of citizens was a fluke and couldn't happen again, then maybe you missed what happened to the mayor of Newark, New Jersey only two weeks later.

Mayor Ras Baraka was arrested by ICE because he wanted to inspect an immigration detention center in his own city of Newark on May 9, 2025. He was there with three members of Congress who had been allowed inside while Baraka was kept in a fenced-in parking lot. When the Congressional members heard authorities wanted to arrest Baraka, they came out of the building and walked with him out of the parking lot to a place outside the fence.

That should have been the end of it.

Instead the federal officers came outside the fence and started a scrum of pushing and shoving. Finally Baraka was handcuffed and taken into custody.

How outrageous was this arresting of a mayor? It was so unheard-of that a local courtroom was opened on a Friday night so Baraka could be heard by a judge and released.

Even worse, in the scrum that took place at the time of Baraka's arrest, two of the Congressional Members were "roughed up" and the third, LaMonica McIver was assaulted according to witnesses. Members of Congress. Roughed up and assaulted.

It's very significant that we heard the details about these things from online influencers, while traditional news only gave watered-down accounts.

Those offences by "local authorities" were worthy of jail-time.

> What we just witnessed was disgusting. If they can treat three members of Congress like that, just imagine how they can treat people on the street each and every day. [21]
>
> *Rep. LaMonica McIver (D-NJ)*

Trump's Department of Justice was just making up facts as it went along. The government representatives made up facts as needed, knowing they would never be held accountable. If McIver successfully defends herself, the charges will just be dropped, with no admission of guilt by DOJ.

Trump is clearly trying to rid Congress of anyone who will speak up and complain about what he is doing.

So what is our response? Let's give him a lot more to worry about by electing more Representatives to Congress who are willing to speak up and take action.

In fact, the only way to stop Trump from doing these clearly illegal acts in violation of the Constitution is to go a step further. We need to make Congress Blue.

The GOP now has a majority in both chambers of Congress, and has been anxious to rubber-stamp whatever Trump has wanted. The Democratic members of Congress have not been much better. They vote to approve Trump's outrageous appointments to Cabinet positions as well as his funding plans.

The cure for both of those problems is to elect more people to the Senate and House who will do what is right. And it won't take very many changes to transform Congress.

Making the House Blue only involves sliding from the current 214 seats to 218 seats. But this should never be about making the minimum or just scraping by.

The amount of self-serving that has become "normal" in Congress has got to be completely removed.

And the Senate needs to start feeling additional pressure towards equalizing the two sides. It would take a mountain of effort to raise enough votes to make the Senate Blue in 2026. But achieving that objective by 2028 is well within reach and should be a definite goal.

The first chance for a Presidential election is in 2028, but the practice for that election will definitely be done here.

Either the destructive proclamations of the MAGA years will be continued, or they will be soundly rejected.

Looking up lost voters and bringing them to the polls will make a huge difference. We talked about this earlier.

Where is the easiest place to make this happen? It can be as close to home as among your relatives. The ones who are adults are often busy and sometimes miss elections. The younger ones may never have gotten in the voting habit, and may not even be registered yet.

You probably already know if they are anti-Trump, and if not, it's easy to chat with them and find out. Even if they live in a different city, you can do the "walk to the mailbox with the absentee ballot" as a video phone call. The treat can be delivered at the next family gathering. It's so easy. And a vote is a vote.

How about with everyone else?

While going about your daily life, just ask your friends, a neighbor, or anyone you happen to be talking to—even if it's just in line at the supermarket:

"By the way, did you happen to vote in the last election?"

If they say no, just add, "So how do you feel about what's happening with food prices and whatever."

If they start complaining, you've got it made. Sympathize. Exchange phone numbers. You just found your Friend.

Closer to the election, make a date for a little voting party. Just meet for pastry and coffee or whatever. At that time have your vote-by-mail ballots in hand, or come with your polling place card in hand so you can go vote together after the little party.

That's it.

With that simple party you may have saved America. Because you brought in one of those 82 million votes that stayed home last time. The game changer. The margin of victory.

The true endgame is to not just get past the disruption of the Trump years. It is to recover our lost rights and laws. It is to live not in a privileged land benefiting only a few. But to protect our families and children as they grow up, sharing the wealth of our great land.

No one is going to come rescue us. We have to do it ourselves.

Chapter

Fourteen

Barack Obama

Will anything be different this year?
What do we need to do?

April 3, 2025
Hamilton College

Let me preface this by saying what everybody knows, which is I have deep differences of opinion with my most immediate successor — who's now president once again. There are a host of policies that we could be discussing where I have strong opinions, but at least for most of my lifetime, I'd say the post-World War II era, there was a broad consensus between Democrats, Republicans, conservatives, liberals around a certain set of rules where we settle our differences.

There are some bonds that transcend party, region, or ideology. There was a creed that we all stuck to. That basic notion of American democracy as embodied in our Constitution and our Bill of Rights said, all of us count, all of us have dignity, all of us have worth that we're going to set up a system in which there's rule of law and separation of powers and an independent judiciary.

There are these freedoms, a freedom of worship and freedom of the press and an assurance that if we go before the law, there will be an impartial process to make decisions. We all stuck to that, more or less. It doesn't mean there weren't corrupt politicians. It doesn't mean there wasn't abuse of power. In society itself, obviously, there were vast differences in terms of access and influence and having a megaphone. But we said, even though that ideal wasn't always observed, that was the right ideal to have.

I do believe that our commitment to those principles has eroded, and I think it eroded in part because the government itself got really big. What that meant is sometimes it felt distant and unresponsive, and rules are a hassle. Some of the rules aren't smart, and people get frustrated. I think part of what happened also is that it's to agree to disagree and have forbearance to people who you don't agree with if they all look like you.

In the United States Senate, when I got there, I was the only African American. There was one Hispanic in the United States Senate. I'm not that old, so this is fairly recently. You had a sense of how different it was by looking at the men's gym in the Senate versus the women's gym. Men's gym, really big, and old guys walking around not wearing enough stuff.

Then the women's gym was basically a modified closet with a bike because there just weren't that many. During that period of our history, I think there was a general sense of, well, if I'm a Dixiecrat, Southern Democrat, if I'm a Republican from up north, if I'm a this or that, have this or that perspective in terms of being fiscally conservative or socially moderate, we all went to the same club and we all talked about the same things.

Then starting around the '60s and '70s, people crashed the party. Now it's a little harder to agree to disagree without being disagreeable if your sense is, well, that person isn't like me. It doesn't look like me, maybe doesn't think exactly the way I think. I'm more prone to feeling attacked or threatened. That, I think, made us a little more tribal in our politics.

Then the economy wasn't working for everybody. Now, that in part, had to do with the fact that government wasn't as responsive as it should have been, and inequality grew. Then finally, media. I think one of the most important aspects of our democratic practice is having a well-informed citizenry which is reliant on a free, objective, effective press, and that started getting attacked.

You combine all those factors together, and we saw them over the course of decades. But obviously, it's gotten a lot worse now. When I watch some of what's going on now, it does not — look, I don't think what we just witnessed in terms of economic policy and tariffs is going to be good for America, but that's a specific policy. I'm more deeply concerned with a federal government that threatens universities if they don't give up students who are exercising their right to free speech.

I am more troubled by the idea that a White House can say to law firms, "If you represent parties that we don't like, we're going to pull all our business or bar you from representing people effectively." That kind of behavior is contrary to the basic compact we have as Americans.

Imagine if I had done any of this. I just want to be clear about this. Imagine if I had pulled Fox News' credentials from the White House press corps. You're laughing, but this is what's happening. Imagine if I had said to law firms that were representing parties that were upset with policies my administration had initiated, that you will not be allowed into government buildings.

We will punish you economically for dissenting from the Affordable Care Act or the Iran deal. We will ferret out students who protest against my policies. It's unimaginable that the same parties that are silent now would have tolerated behavior like that from me, or a whole bunch of my predecessors.

I say this not on a partisan basis. This has to do with something more precious, which is who are we as a country and what values do we stand for? Now, this is not just an abstraction. I think this is one of the challenges that we have, and I saw this even before the last election. I think people tend to think, oh, democracy, rule of law, independent judiciary, freedom of the press. That's all abstract stuff because it's not affecting the price of eggs. Well, you know what? It's about to affect the price of eggs.

One of the things that has distinguished us in the past has been this basic idea that we are a rules-based society. What that means is that you know what? I can support one candidate instead of another, and I don't have to worry that the police are going to come harass me or my customers. That's what happens in other places. That's what happens in Russia.

We take for granted the idea that we don't have to pay bribes or hire somebody's cousin in order to get a business permit. That's how we built the economy we did. That's why this place worked. It has very concrete impacts on all of our lives. This is the first time I've been speaking publicly for a while. I've been watching a little bit.

Yeah. Let me just close this portion of my remarks by saying it is up to all of us to fix this. It's not going to be because somebody comes and saves you. The most important office in this democracy is the citizen, the ordinary person who says, no, that's not right. I do think one of the reasons that our commitment to democratic ideals has eroded is that we got pretty comfortable and complacent.

It has been easy during most of our lifetimes to say you are a progressive or say you are for social justice or say you're for free speech and not have to pay a price for it. Now we're at one of those moments where, you know what? It's not enough just to say you're for something; you may actually have to do something and possibly sacrifice a little bit.

Barack Obama

APPENDIX

Index

Annotations

[1] Spenser Humphrey " 'We're citizens!': Oklahoma City family traumatized after ICE raids home, but they weren't suspects" *KFOR,* April 29, 2025. Retrieved on 4/29/25 from https://kfor.com/news/local/were-citizens-oklahoma-city-family-traumatized-after-ice-raids-home-but-they-werent-suspects.

[2] Billal Rahman "ICE Agents Realize They Arrested Wrong Teen, Say 'Take Him Anyway'" *Newsweek,* April 15, 2025. Retrieved on May 15, 2025 from https://www.newsweek.com/merwil-gutierrez-ice-wrong-teen-el-salvador-2059783.

[3] Jose Olivares "US citizen wrongfully arrested by border patrol in Arizona held for nearly 10 days" *The Guardian,* April 21 2025. Retrieved on May 15, 2025 from

https://www.theguardian.com/us-news/2025/apr/20/us-citizen-jose-hermosillo-border-patrol.
[4] Martín González Gómez, Alicia Parlapiano, Jasmine C. Lee and Lily Boyce "How Every Senator Voted to Confirm Kristi Noem as Secretary of Homeland Security" *The New York Times,* January 25, 2025. Retrieved on June 5, 2025 from https://www.nytimes.com/interactive/2025/01/25/us/politics/noem-senate-confirmation-vote.html
[5] James M. Lindsay "The 2024 Election by the Numbers" *Council on Foreign Relations,* December 18, 2024. Retrieved on May12, 2025 from https://www.cfr.org/article/2024-election-numbers.
[6] U.S. Census Bureau "2024 Presidential Election Voting and Registration Tables Now Available" *U.S. Census Bureau,* April 30, 2025. Retrieved on May 12, 2025 from https://www.census.gov/newsroom/press-releases/2025/2024-presidential-election-voting-registration-tables.html
[7] Hilary Cadigan "Alexandria Ocasio-Cortez Learned Her Most Important Lessons from Restaurants" *Bon Appetit,* November 7, 2018. Retrieved on May 22, 2025 from https://www.bonappetit.com/story/alexandria-ocasio-cortez-lessons-from-restaurants.
[8] Timothy Bella "A viral photo showed former NBA star Delonte West homeless. Mark Cuban found him and picked him up." *The Washington Post,* September 29, 2020. Retrieved on May 22, 2025 from https://www.washingtonpost.com/nation/2020/09/29/mark-cuban-delonte-west.

[9] Rebecca Morin "Endorsing Clinton, Mark Cuban calls Trump a 'jagoff'" *Politico,* July 30, 2016. Retrieved on August 9, 2025 from https://www.politico.com/story/2016/07/mark-cuban-hillary-clinton-donald-trump-226472.

[10] Lois Beckett "LA Times editor resigns after owner blocks presidential endorsement" *The Guardian,* October 23, 2024. Retrieved on May 10, 2025 from https://www.theguardian.com/media/2024/oct/23/la-times-editor-resigns-presidential-endorsement.

[11] Hadas Gold and Brian Stelter, "Washington Post won't endorse candidate in 2024 presidential election after Bezos decision" *CNN,* October 25, 2024. Retrieved on May 10, 2025 from https://www.cnn.com/2024/10/25/media/washington-post-wont-endorse-presidential-candidate.

[12] Zachary Basu, "Trump's billion-dollar settlement spree" *Axios,* July 30, 2025. Retrieved on August 2, 2025 from https://www.axios.com/2025/07/30/trump-harvard-settlement-dei-lawsuit.

[13] Virginia Heffernan "Liberal Media in Crisis? Not The MeidasTouch. It's Bigger than Rogan." *The New Republic,* April 23, 2025. Retrieved on May 27, 2025 from https://newrepublic.com/article/194187/meidastouch-ben-meiselas-liberal-media-bigger-rogan.

[14] Mascaro, Lisa "Speaker Johnson tells GOP lawmakers to skip town halls after an onslaught of protests" *AP,* March 4, 2025. Retrieved on April 2, 2026, from https://apnews.com/article/town-halls-musk-doge-trump-gop-749d91ea516284057e4c7bcb1615527e.

[15] "Buying Time 2025 – Wisconsin" *Brenan Center for Justice,* April 4, 2025. Retreived on March 3, 2026 from https://www.brennancenter.org/our-work/research-reports/buying-time-2025-wisconsin

[16] Neal K. Katyal and George T. Conway III "Trump's Appointment of the Acting Attorney General Is Unconstitutional" *The New York Times,* November 8, 2018. Retrieved on May 27, 2025 from https://www.nytimes.com/2018/11/08/opinion/trump-attorney-general-sessions-unconstitutional.html

[17] Natasha Bertrand "How a veteran's secret podcast put her in the Trump administration's crosshairs" *Politico,* June 28, 2020. Retrieved on May 31, 2025 from https://www.politico.com/news/2020/06/28/veteran-secret-podcast-trump-administrations-crosshairs-342332.

[18] Chris Murphy "Murphy To Secretary Of Homeland Security Kristi Noem: Your Department Is Out Of Control" May 08, 2025. These remarks were presented by the Senator at a Senate subcommittee hearing in Congress. Retrieved on May 11, 2025 from https://www.murphy.senate.gov/newsroom/press-releases/murphy-to-secretary-of-homeland-security-kristi-noem-your-department-is-out-of-control.

[19] Duke Law Magazine staff "Focused on voting" *Duke Law Magazine,* Winter 2021, Vol. 40, no. 1. Retrieved on May 29, 2025 from https://magazine.law.duke.edu/elias93_conversation

[20] Evan Thomas "Inside the Beltway but Out of the Loop" *The New York Times,* April 27, 1997. Retrieved on

May 24, 2025 from
https://archive.nytimes.com/www.nytimes.com/books/98/09/13/specials/reich-cabinet.html

[21] Ry Rivard "New Jersey Mayor Ras Baraka arrested at ICE facility" *Politico,* May 9, 2025. Retrieved on May 9, 2025 from
https://www.politico.com/news/2025/05/09/new-jersey-mayor-ras-baraka-ice-00339287.

Made in the USA
Las Vegas, NV
11 June 2026

48679029R00075